AF448148

Adventures in Scripture for Kids: Exploring the Fruit of the Spirit

Lorie Eubank

GTO Publishing Solutions, LLC.

Copyright © 2024 by Lorie Eubank

All rights reserved.

No portion of this book may be reproduced in any form without written permission from the publisher or author, except as permitted by U.S. copyright law.

Contents

Dedication

To my children, Thadyn, Geordyn, and Oslyne thank you for your support and encouragement while I worked on this series. I couldn't have done it without you. I am so honored to be your mom and walk this life journey with you.

To my Sunday school students, especially those who were with me in the early days of 2002 when I began my journey teaching and helping in the Children's Ministry. Jonathan, there will never be a time that I don't think of you when discussing the Red Sea. Aaron, Sean, Tiffany, Lauren, Joshua, Wesley, Emily, Jack, Luke, Bryant, Sharon and Shirley, and so many more of you, thank you for inspiring me to learn more and grow in a deeper relationship with the Lord so that I could be a better teacher.

To all of those children who grew with me through the years to love the Lord, I pray the seeds sown in the classes will continue to grow and bear fruit in your lives. May your children walk in the fellowship and relationship with the Lord and be a light just as you have been.

Introduction: Setting Off on a Fruitful Adventure

Greetings, young adventurers!

You might wonder where we're heading as we begin this new journey. No, it's not a trek through a dense forest or a hike up the steepest mountain. This is a unique adventure that focuses on developing heart character and exploring the treasures that exist within us. These treasures, called the Fruit of the Spirit, are wonderful qualities we can all nurture and grow.

What are the Fruit of the Spirit?

Perhaps you've heard of them, or maybe they're entirely new to you. Either way, you're in for a treat! The Fruit of the Spirit isn't like the fruit we eat—apples, oranges, or bananas. Instead, they're like inner qualities or virtues that we can cultivate in our lives.

They are:

1. Love

2. Joy

3. Peace

4. Patience

5. Kindness

6. Goodness

7. Faithfulness

8. Gentleness

9. Self-control

Each of these is like a badge of honor, a sign that we are growing and becoming better people. They are mentioned in the Bible, in Galatians, where the Apostle Paul lists these nine virtues to guide and inspire us.

Why are they important?

Now, think about a garden for a moment. Imagine it filled with blooming flowers, tall trees, and fluttering butterflies. But if the gardener doesn't tend to the plants or water them regularly, they might wither away. Similarly, our hearts are like that garden, and the Fruit of the Spirit are the vibrant flowers and trees within. When we nurture and care for these virtues, our lives become more fulfilling, more joyful, and more harmonious.

But why, you ask? Why are these nine virtues so crucial?

For starters, they shape our character. Character is like our identity, the very essence of who we are. The more we embrace and practice these virtues, the more we become individuals others look up to and admire.

For instance, when we practice patience, we learn to wait our turn, to listen more than we speak, and to understand others. We spread warmth and light with kindness, making someone's day brighter. Joy allows us to celebrate the little things in life, and love lets us care for others deeply.

How they help us in our daily lives

In our everyday life, we encounter numerous challenges, from difficult math problems to disagreements with friends. Sometimes, things don't go as planned, and we feel upset or frustrated. It's natural. But this is where the Fruit of the Spirit can come to our aid!

1. **Love**: When we act with love, we show others we care about their feelings. This means listening to them, supporting them, and being there when they need us.

2. **Joy**: Life is filled with ups and downs, but by embracing joy, we can find happiness in the smallest of things, like a beautiful sunset or a kind gesture from a friend.

3. **Peace**: In moments of chaos or disagreement, seeking peace helps us calm down, think clearly, and find solutions without getting upset.

4. **Patience**: Whether waiting for our turn in a game or trying to understand a tricky subject in school, patience reminds us that everything has its time.

5. **Kindness**: A simple act of kindness, like sharing our toys or helping someone, can brighten someone's day and make us feel good too.

6. **Goodness**: By choosing to do what's right, even when no one is watching, we develop integrity.

7. **Faithfulness**: Sticking to our promises, honoring our word when we say we will do something, and being reliable makes us trustworthy.

8. **Gentleness**: Instead of getting angry or raising our voices, gentleness teaches us to handle situations softly and kindly.

9. **Self-control**: From not eating all the cookies at once to staying calm when we're upset, self-control guides us to make balanced decisions.

By understanding and practicing the Fruit of the Spirit, our daily life becomes smoother. We can handle challenges better, build stronger friendships, and, most importantly, grow internally, becoming wiser and more understanding with each passing day.

So, are you ready to take a leap of faith into this journey? As we explore each fruit in the chapters ahead, we'll discover stories, examples, and fun activities to help you understand and nurture these virtues in your life. It promises to be a rewarding expedition where we learn, grow, and change for the better together.

Let's set off on this fruitful adventure and explore the treasures that lie within our hearts!

Chapter 1: Love

"And now these three remain: faith, hope, and love. But the greatest of these is love." - 1 Corinthians 13:13

Discovering Love

What is love? It's a simple word, but it holds so much power. Love isn't just a feeling; it's an action, a decision, and a way of living. Love is when Mom or Dad tucks you into bed at night with a sweet story or your sibling shares their favorite toy with you. It's the warmth you feel when surrounded by your family and friends, laughing, playing, and making memories together.

What does love look and feel like?

Imagine a warm, comforting blanket wrapped around you on a chilly day. That's love. It's the feeling you get when Grandma bakes your favorite cookies just because she knows they make you smile. Love is in the tiny moments, like a smile from a friend, a hug from Mom, or a high-five from Dad after you've done something amazing. Love can be seen in the way your teacher patiently explains something until you understand or when a friend helps you when you're feeling down.

Bible stories about love

The Bible is filled with stories that shine a light on love in its purest form. Remember the story of Ruth and Naomi? Ruth's unwavering love for her mother-in-law, Naomi, is a beautiful example of dedication and loyalty.

Ruth and Naomi: Ruth's determination to stay with Naomi, her mother-in-law, after the death of her husband is a picture of steadfast love. She told Naomi, "Where you go, I will go; where you stay, I will stay." (Ruth 1:16)

Another powerful story is of David and Jonathan, whose friendship was so strong that they were like brothers. Their bond showed that love could be found not only in family ties but also in profound friendships.

David and Jonathan: Their friendship transcended family ties, politics, and even threats to David's life. It's said in the scriptures, "Jonathan loved David as he loved himself." (1 Samuel 18:3)

My personal favorite, probably because it was the first scripture I ever learned, was the love God had for each of us. No matter who you are or what mistake you have made, God loves you.

God gave His Son: Perhaps the most profound expression of love is noted in John 3:16-17 (NLT), "For God so loved the world that He gave His one and only Son, that whoever believes in him shall not perish but have eternal life. God sent his Son into the world not to condemn the world, but to save the world through him." This embodies the essence of sacrificial love.

How Jesus showed love

Jesus is the ultimate example of love. He healed the sick, fed the hungry, and spent time with those society had cast aside. He welcomed children, taught lessons of kindness, and even washed the feet of His disciples. But His most significant act of love is laying down His life for all of us so we might have eternal life. Jesus once said, *"Greater love has no one than this: to lay down one's life for one's friends."* And He did exactly that for us.

Jesus's life is a testament to unwavering love. Here are some of the ways He showed His great love:

1. **Healing the Sick:** Jesus did not differentiate based on status. Whether it was a leper or a leader's daughter, He showed love by healing them.

2. **Feeding Thousands:** With just five loaves and two fishes, Jesus fed a crowd of five thousand, showing love and compassion for the hungry masses.

3. **Embracing Children:** When the disciples tried to shoo away mothers bringing their children for blessings, Jesus said, "Let the little children come to me, and do not hinder them." (Matthew 19:14)

4. **The Last Supper:** In one of His final acts before His

crucifixion, Jesus washed the feet of His disciples, a task typically reserved for servants. This humble act was a demonstration of servant leadership and profound love. He was living out the example that He wanted them to follow, not the washing of feet, but the act of serving others.

5. **Sacrifice on the Cross:** Jesus's crucifixion is the ultimate act or example of His love. By sacrificing Himself, He paved the way for humanity's salvation. No other sacrifice would ever be required to atone or forgive sin. He was the perfect Lamb, provided by God to forgive us of our sins forever. All we have to do now is ASK God to forgive us of our sins, and He is faithful to forgive us.

Other Expressions of Love

Love isn't limited to serious moments; it's also in play! Think about the times you are playing with your friends. Sharing toys, taking turns, and being there for one another all stem from love. When you create games that everyone can enjoy or make sure no one feels left out, you're showcasing love in the purest childlike manner.

Here are three ways you can show love to one another, drawing inspiration from the way Jesus shows love:

1. **Unconditional Acceptance and Kindness**

- **What Jesus Did:** Jesus associated with and showed kindness to people society rejected or looked down upon, such as tax collectors, lepers, and sinners. He taught that everyone deserves love and understanding.

- **What You Can Do:** You can demonstrate this type of love by being inclusive and welcoming to all peers, regardless of their differences or backgrounds. For instance, if you notice a classmate sitting alone during lunchtime, you might invite that classmate to join your group, ensuring no one feels left out or isolated.

2. Forgiveness and Reconciliation

- **What Jesus Did:** Jesus emphasized the importance of forgiveness on multiple occasions. One of the most powerful examples is when He forgave those who crucified Him, saying, "Father, forgive them, for they do not know what they are doing" (Luke 23:34).

- **What You Can Do:** If another child inadvertently hurts you, whether through words or actions, you can choose to forgive, emphasizing the importance of your relationship over holding onto grudges. For instance, if two friends disagree about a toy, rather than holding a grudge, one could say, "It's okay, I forgive you. Let's find a way to share."

3. Selfless Service and Generosity

- ○ **What Jesus Did:** Jesus washed the feet of His disciples (John 13:1-17), an act of humble service, signifying that no task is beneath us when done out of love for others.

- ○ **What You Can Do:** You can put others' needs ahead of your own. For example, if you see a peer struggling with their homework or an art project, you might offer help or share your materials. Another instance might be when someone willingly gives up their turn on the swing so another child can have a chance to enjoy it.

Following these examples not only helps you grow stronger bonds of friendship but also lays the foundation for cultivating Christ-like love as you grow.

Fun activities: making love-filled crafts

Craft time can be a fun way to express love. Think about the joy of creating a handmade card for Mom on Mother's Day or a special drawing for Dad's office. Every stroke of the brush, every color you choose, and every glittery sticker you add is an expression of your love. These crafts are special because they come straight from the heart.

Another delightful activity is creating a "Love Jar." You only need an empty jar, some colored paper, and pens. Write down little notes of things you love about your family members, fold them, and place them in the jar. On days when someone needs a bit of cheering up, they can pull out a note and be reminded of the love surrounding them.

These are just a small example of how you can show love to others. Flip the switch and use your creative imagination to think of a few ways that your love for them might bless others. Sometimes, for a family, it might be as simple as telling them you love them. For a friend, it may just be you playing with them or saying an encouraging word. For others, it could be as simple as recognizing they are there and including them in what you are doing.

Heartwarming moments with family and friends

Recall a time when you felt incredibly loved. Maybe it was your birthday, and everyone came together to celebrate you. Or perhaps it was a quiet moment with your family, watching a movie or reading a book together. Love is present in both grand gestures and silent moments. It's in how your friend listens to you, how your pet curls up beside you, or when your family comes together to celebrate special occasions.

Spreading Love Every Day

Love isn't just a one-time thing; it's a daily choice. Each day presents opportunities to showcase love in all we do.

Small Acts of Love

Simple acts, like helping set the dinner table, holding the door open for someone, or sharing your snack, are ways we can show love daily. It's about putting others before ourselves and making the world a little brighter with our actions.

Loving our pets and toys

Our pets, whether fluffy, scaly, or feathery, bring so much joy to our lives. We can express our love by caring for them, feeding them, playing with them, and giving them cuddles.

Similarly, taking care of our toys, treating them gently, and even occasionally giving them a "spa day" (read: cleaning day) are ways we love the inanimate yet cherished members of our playroom.

Saying kind words to our friends

"Thank you," "You're awesome," "I appreciate you"—words have power. When we use kind words, we're spreading love in the most vocal way. It takes only a moment to compliment a friend or thank someone.

As we venture into the next chapter on the Fruit of Joy, we must remember that Love leads. If we let love lead our every action and decision, we will reflect the love of Christ in all we do. Like love, if we choose Joy, even when we are not happy about everything going on around us, it will help us get through to the other side.

Chapter 2: Joy

"Though you have not seen Him, you love Him, and even though you do not see Him now, you believe in Him and are filled with an inexpressible and glorious joy." - 1 Peter 1:8

Finding Joy

Have you ever watched the sunrise, painting the sky with shades of pink and gold, and felt a warm glow inside? Or heard a joke so funny you couldn't stop laughing? That's the feeling of joy. It's more than just being happy because something good happened. Joy is a deep-rooted emotion, like a bubbling spring in our hearts, that can always be present, even during challenging times.

Joy vs. just being happy

Happiness is a wonderful feeling, but it often comes from external events. Maybe you're happy because you got a new toy or because it's your birthday. Joy, on the other hand, goes deeper. It's an inner feeling that doesn't always depend on what's happening around us. While happiness might be like a gentle stream, joy is like a powerful, ever-present ocean wave. You can have joy even on days when things don't go as planned, reminding you that every cloud has a silver lining.

Bible Stories of Celebration and Joy

The Bible, our guidebook for life, is filled with stories that teach us about joy. These stories teach us that joy can be found in unexpected places and moments.

The Birth of Jesus (Luke 2:1-20): The story of the Birth of Jesus, often referred to as the Nativity begins with Mary and Joseph traveling from Nazareth to Bethlehem due to a decree from Caesar Augustus that required everyone to return to their ancestral towns to be registered. With Bethlehem crowded and accommodations scarce, they found shelter in a stable. There, Mary gave birth to Jesus, wrapping Him in swaddling cloths and laying Him in a manger. This humble beginning contrasts sharply with the significance of Jesus' birth, symbolizing the approachability and humility of Christ coming into the world.

On the night of Jesus' birth, an angel of the Lord appeared to shepherds in the nearby fields, illuminating the darkness with the glory of God. The angel announced the joyous news of the Savior's birth, a message of great joy for all people, indicating that Jesus came not just for the elite or the religious, but for everyone, from the humble shepherds to future generations across the world. Suddenly, a multitude of heavenly hosts joined the angel, praising God and saying, "Glory to God in the highest, and on earth peace, goodwill toward men!" Moved by this divine revelation, the shepherds went to Bethlehem to see the newborn Jesus, confirming the angel's message. They left glorifying and praising God, spreading the word about what they had witnessed. The joy in this story emanates from the fulfillment of ancient prophecies and the incarnation of God's love in human form, offering hope, redemption, and a deep, abiding joy to all humankind.

Paul and Silas in Prison (Acts 16:25-34): The account of Paul and Silas where they find themselves imprisoned in Philippi after being severely beaten for casting a spirit out of a slave girl, leading to a loss of income for her masters. Instead of succumbing to despair, Paul and Silas choose to engage in prayer and sing hymns to God, even in the depths of the night, their bodies wounded and confined in the innermost part of the prison. This act of worship in the face of dire circumstances demonstrates an extraordinary depth of faith and an unshakable joy in their belief in God's sovereignty, regardless of their physical conditions.

Remarkably, their joy and faith set the stage for a miraculous event: a sudden earthquake shakes the prison, opening the doors and loosening the chains that bind the prisoners. This supernatural occurrence catches the attention of the jailer, who, fearing that the prisoners had escaped, was about to take his own life. Paul intervenes, assuring him that all the prisoners were present. This leads to the pivotal moment where the jailer, moved by the integrity and the unwavering faith of Paul and Silas, seeks salvation, asking, "Sirs, what must I do to be saved?" They respond with the simple yet profound truth, "Believe in the Lord Jesus, and you will be saved, you and your household." The story culminates in the jailer washing their wounds and being baptized along with his entire household, rejoicing in his newfound faith.

This story beautifully illustrates how joy, rooted in faith, can transcend the most challenging circumstances, leading not only to personal freedom but also impacting the lives of others. The joy Paul and Silas exhibited in their darkest hour became a powerful testimony, leading to the transformation and salvation of the jailer and his family. It serves as a compelling reminder of the powerful impact that a joyous faith in God can have, capable of bringing light to the darkest places and turning despair into hope.

The Healing of the Lame Man by Peter and John (Acts 3:1-10): Peter and John encounter a man lame from birth at the Beautiful Gate of the temple in Jerusalem, where he was placed daily to beg for alms or money. When he sees Peter and John about to enter the temple, he asks them for money. Instead of offering silver or gold, Peter, filled with the Holy Spirit, offers something far more powerful. He commands the man in the name of Jesus Christ of Nazareth to rise up and walk. Peter then takes the man by the right hand and helps him up. Instantly, the man's feet and ankles become strong, enabling him to stand, walk, and even leap for the first time in his life. The man enters the temple courts with them, walking, jumping, and praising God.

This miraculous healing serves not only as a testament to the power of faith in Jesus Christ but also illustrates the transformative joy that comes with experiencing God's work firsthand. The lame man's joy is spontaneous and unrestrained, drawing the attention of all those present in the temple. His reaction to the miracle—leaping and praising God—captures the essence of joy that cannot be contained. This scene creates a ripple effect among the witnesses, leading to awe and wonder about the power and compassion of God.

The story of the healing of the lame man underscores the theme that true joy and fulfillment come not from material possessions but from the presence and power of God in one's life. The man's leap is not just a physical action but a symbol of the spiritual liberation and joy that comes with faith and healing in Jesus' name. It highlights how the acts of faith by believers can lead to miraculous outcomes, bringing joy not only to the recipients of God's grace but also to the broader community, inspiring faith and praise to God.

As we discussed in the last chapter on Love, God loves us so much that He gave His Son as a final sacrifice so we no longer had to live under judgment or condemnation.   When we repent, God is faithful to forgive. Not only does His forgiveness restore us to Him, but because we are restored to His presence, His Joy becomes our strength to be strong and not sin again. Or at least the Holy Spirit tries to encourage us to make the right choices.

Sharing Joy Daily

Every day presents countless opportunities to experience and spread joy. But what's powerful about the Fruit of Joy is its ability to magnify and reverberate, especially when shared.

The adage "A joy shared is a joy doubled" underscores a fundamental human experience. Emotions, especially positive ones like joy, have a contagious quality. Consider the simple act of smiling at a stranger on the street. While it might seem insignificant to you, it can light up someone else's day, prompting them to carry that warmth forward. This ripple effect can turn a single act of joy into a cascade of happiness, affecting countless individuals.

But why does sharing joy amplify it? Well, humans are inherently social beings. We thrive on connection, understanding, and shared experiences. When we are in a state of joy and choose to share it, we not only validate our own feelings but also invite others to partake in that emotional state. It's like lighting candles – one flame can ignite countless others without diminishing its own brightness.

Walking in the Fruit of Joy also means recognizing that joy isn't just in grand gestures or significant life events. It's in the daily, often overlooked moments. It's in a child's laughter, the aroma of a freshly baked pie, a favorite song playing on the radio, or even the feeling of the sun's rays on a cold day. When we acknowledge these moments and share them – be it through a story, a gesture, or an act of kindness – we create avenues for others to recognize and cherish their joy-filled moments too.

Moreover, sharing joy serves as a reminder that happiness isn't finite. There isn't a set amount of joy in the world that gets depleted with sharing. On the contrary, it's an ever-growing, boundless resource. The more we tap into it and distribute it, the richer and more widespread it becomes. Joy is a choice; you can choose joy to overcome other emotions. It finding something good in the mundane.

So, in the journey of life, as we strive to walk daily in the Fruit of Joy, it's essential to remember its intrinsic communal nature. Our individual joy can become a collective experience, reinforcing connections, building communities, and reminding everyone of the beauty that life holds, one joyful moment at a time.

Something as simple as a smile can spread joy. When you smile at someone, more often than not, they'll smile back. And that simple exchange can brighten someone's day. The same goes for laughter. Sharing a funny story or joke can bring joy to a whole group, making the moment memorable.

Finding joy in simple things

Sometimes, the simplest things can bring the most joy. The fluttering of a butterfly, the aroma of freshly baked cookies, the feel of soft grass beneath your feet—these are all moments of joy waiting to be discovered. Every day is an opportunity to create joy-filled memories. Whether it's a family picnic, a day at the park, or just sitting together reading a book, these moments become treasures of joy that we can revisit time and again.

As we journey through life, let's remember to seek out and spread joy in every corner. Because, in the end, it's these joy-filled days that make our lives truly rich and meaningful. As we continue our journey in learning more about the Fruit of the Spirit, leading with Love, and sharing Joy, take us to walk in Peace.

Chapter 3: Peace

"Peace I leave with you; my peace I give you. I do not give to you as the world gives. Do not let your hearts be troubled and do not be afraid." - John 14:27

Understanding Peace

What does "peace" mean to you? Some might think of a serene landscape, a calm lake with birds chirping, or maybe a quiet evening with family. Peace isn't just the absence of noise or trouble; it's a deep sense of calm and contentment, regardless of what's happening around us.

What it feels like to be peaceful

Close your eyes for a moment and imagine you're in your favorite place, perhaps a garden or your cozy bed. There's no loud noise, no rush, just you feeling safe and relaxed. That's peace. It's a feeling that everything is alright, even if it's just for that moment. When we're peaceful, our hearts feel light, our thoughts are clear, and we feel secure.

Bible stories about finding calm

The Bible has many stories that teach us about finding calm amidst chaos.

Elijah and the Still Small Voice (1 Kings 19:11-13): It unfolds after Elijah's dramatic victory over the prophets of Baal on Mount Carmel, where he demonstrated the power of the one true God. Following this triumph, Queen Jezebel threatened Elijah's life, driving him into the wilderness, where he fell into despair, even asking God to take his life. God led Elijah to Mount Horeb, also known as Mount Sinai, to seek God's presence.

While on the mountain, Elijah experienced a series of powerful natural events. God instructed him to stand on the mountain as the Lord was about to pass by. A great and strong wind tore through the mountains, shattering rocks, but God was not in the wind. After the wind, there was an earthquake, but God was not in the earthquake. Following the earthquake came a fire, but God was not in the fire. After the fire, there was a gentle whisper, a still small voice, where Elijah found God's presence. In response, Elijah covered his face with his cloak and stood at the cave entrance, ready to listen to God.

This story emphasizes the contrast between God's dramatic manifestations and His quiet, subtle ways of communication. It teaches the importance of seeking God not only in extraordinary events but also in the calm, still moments of life. The "still small voice" symbolizes God's gentle, reassuring presence that guides and comforts us in times of trouble and uncertainty. It reminds us that God's guidance often comes in quiet, unexpected ways, encouraging us to listen attentively for His direction amidst the noise and distractions of life. In listening and waiting on God, He will fill you with His peace.

Daniel in the Lion's Den (Daniel 6): Daniel, a devout servant of God, was among the Jewish captives in Babylon. Due to his exceptional wisdom and integrity, Daniel gained favor with King Darius, which led to jealousy among other officials. They conspired against Daniel, manipulating the king into issuing a decree that, for thirty days, no one could pray to any god or human except to the king himself. Daniel, unwavering in his faith, continued to pray openly to God three times a day.

The conspirators reported Daniel to King Darius, who, bound by his own decree, was forced to order Daniel's punishment: being thrown into a den of lions. Despite his anguish, the king hoped Daniel's God would rescue him. The next morning, Darius hurried to the den and was overjoyed to find Daniel unharmed. Daniel declared that God had sent an angel to shut the lions' mouths because he was found innocent in God's sight. Astonished by the miraculous deliverance, King Darius then issued a new decree, proclaiming that all his people should tremble and fear before the God of Daniel, who is the living God, enduring forever.

The story reminds us of the triumph of faith and integrity over deceit and envy. It teaches that unwavering trust in God can lead to His divine protection and deliverance from seemingly unbeatable challenges. Daniel's story is a testament to the power of steadfast faith and the peace that comes from knowing God is always in control, even in the most difficult situations.

Jesus Calms the Storm (Mark 4:35-41): It begins with Jesus suggesting to His disciples that they cross to the other side of the Sea of Galilee. As they sailed, a fierce storm unexpectedly arose, with high winds and waves so intense they began filling the boat with water. Despite the chaos and fear of the disciples, Jesus remained asleep on a cushion in the stern of the ship, undisturbed by the tumult around Him.

Fearing for their lives, the disciples woke Jesus, asking Him if He cared that they were about to perish. Jesus stood up, rebuked the wind, and said to the sea, "Peace! Be still!" The storm immediately ceased, and there was a great calm. He then turned to His disciples and questioned their faith, asking why they were so afraid and if they still had no faith. The disciples were left in awe, marveling at Jesus' power and questioning among themselves who He was, that even the wind and the sea obeyed Him.

This story highlights several important points. Firstly, it demonstrates Jesus' authority over nature, affirming His divine nature and power. Secondly, it addresses the theme of faith, challenging the disciples (and the readers) to trust in Jesus even in the most terrifying circumstances. The calming of the storm serves as a metaphor for the peace Jesus brings amid life's metaphorical storms. It reassures us that, with faith in Jesus, we can find peace and security regardless of the chaos and challenges we might face in the world.

Jesus and peace

Our Savior, Jesus Christ, is often called the "Prince of Peace." Throughout his life, Jesus exemplified what it means to have inner peace. When a furious storm rocked the boat he was in, Jesus remained calm, even asleep, amidst the panic. Upon waking, he commanded the winds and waves to be still, bringing peace to the scared disciples and the turbulent sea.

His teachings, too, emphasize the importance of peace. He taught us to love our enemies, to turn the other cheek, and to live in harmony with everyone. Through His teachings and actions, Jesus showed that true peace comes from trusting God and loving others.

Peaceful Playtime

While peace often feels like quietness, there are many activities and games that can help us understand and cherish this wonderful feeling better.

Relaxing activities and crafts

Crafts have a special way of focusing our energies and helping us find calm. Consider creating a "Peaceful Place" collage: gather magazines, colored papers, and glue. Cut out images that represent peace to you, then stick them on a larger piece of paper. This collage can be a daily reminder of what peace looks like.

Another calming activity is drawing or coloring. There are many coloring books available with intricate designs and patterns. Coloring can be therapeutic, helping our minds focus and relax.

Talking about peaceful moments

Remember the last time you felt completely at peace? Maybe it was after listening to a beautiful song or spending a day with family. Sharing these moments helps us recognize the value of peace in our lives. It's also an opportunity to learn from others about what brings them peace and tranquility.

Keeping Calm Every Day

Every day might not be peaceful, but we can find peace every day. Let's explore some practical ways to maintain calm in our daily lives.

Breathing exercises for kids

Breathing deeply and slowly can be a great way to find calm quickly. Try this exercise:

1. Sit or lie down comfortably.

2. Close your eyes and take a deep breath in through your nose, counting to four.

3. Hold your breath for a count of four.

4. Slowly exhale through your mouth for a count of four.

Repeating this a few times can help clear your mind and calm your heartbeat.

Peaceful bedtime routines

A calm evening can set the stage for a peaceful night. Consider these steps for a tranquil bedtime routine:

1. Dim the lights an hour before sleep.

2. Listen to calming music or read a gentle story.

3. Share with your family one good thing that happened during the day.

4. Say a prayer, thanking God for His protection and asking for a peaceful night.

Handling disagreements with friends

Conflicts can disrupt our peace but are also opportunities to practice maintaining calm. When disagreements arise:

1. Listen to your friend without interrupting.

2. Speak calmly, expressing how you feel.

3. Look for a solution together; remember, disagreements are okay, but arguing is not.

In the end, peace is a gift from God. By understanding it, experiencing it in different ways, and practicing it daily, we can truly appreciate this precious fruit of the Spirit. As we grow, remember to seek peace, share it with others, and treasure those calm skies and quiet nights. As we continue learning more about the Fruit of the Spirit, leading with Love, sharing Joy, walking in Peace, and persevering in Patience.

Chapter 4: Patience

"But those who wait on the Lord shall renew their strength; they shall mount up with wings like eagles, they shall run and not be weary, they shall walk and not faint." - Isaiah 40:31

Learning About Patience

When you hear the word "patience," what comes to mind? Perhaps sitting and waiting for your turn at a game or looking at the sky, waiting for the rain to stop so you can play outside. While all these moments require patience, it's more than just waiting. Patience is a quiet strength, a gentle perseverance, and the ability to remain hopeful even when things don't go as planned. It's like patience is a superpower.

Why patience is more than just waiting

So, think about that seed you plant in a garden. Planting it is just the beginning. Once it's in the ground, your job isn't just to sit on a chair and stare at it, hoping it'll turn into a beautiful flower overnight. Nope, that's not how it works!

Instead, you give that little seed some TLC – tender loving care. You make sure it gets a drink of water when it's thirsty. You shield it from those sneaky bugs that might want a nibble. And you always ensure it gets plenty of sunshine.

Now, here's the cool part. While you're doing all these things, you also have this amazing trust deep inside you. Even if you can't see anything happening right away, you believe that one day, that tiny seed will sprout and grow into something beautiful.

That belief and care you put in and the time you wait all mixed together? That's what we call patience. It's not just about waiting; it's about believing, caring, and hoping all at the same time. Remember, great things take time, just like how it takes time for that seed to blossom. So, the next time you're getting a little antsy waiting for something, think about that seed and remember that patience is so much more than just waiting. It's a journey filled with care and hope.

Bible stories of waiting and rewards

Have you ever had to wait for something so long that it felt like forever? Well, some of the heroes in the Bible waited for many, many years, and their stories teach us a thing or two about patience.

Noah Builds the Ark (Genesis 6:9-22; 7-8): The story of Noah and the Ark, found in the book of Genesis, is a powerful narrative of unwavering faith and patience. God, grieved by the wickedness of humanity, decides to cleanse the earth with a great flood. However, Noah finds favor in the eyes of the Lord due to his righteousness amidst a corrupt world. God instructs Noah to build an ark, a massive vessel capable of holding his family and representatives of all animal species. Despite the monumental nature of this task and the absence of any visible sign of a flood (as it had never rained on the earth before), Noah embarks on this daunting project with steadfast obedience and patience.

For approximately 120 years, Noah diligently worked on the ark, enduring what can be imagined as widespread doubt and ridicule from those around him. This period of building is not just a testament to Noah's patience but also his profound trust in God's promise and timing. When the floodwaters finally come, Noah's faith and patience are vindicated. The ark serves as the vessel of salvation for his family and the animal kingdom, preserving life to repopulate the earth post-flood. Noah's story emphasizes the virtues of patience and obedience to God's will, teaching us the value of trusting in God's plan, even when it unfolds over long periods and in ways that might be difficult to understand or accept.

Can you imagine being told to build a gigantic boat, even when there was no sign of rain? Now, here's the kicker: Noah spent *120 years* building that ark and waiting for the flood. That's longer than the oldest person you probably know! But he trusted God, stayed patient, and in the end, he and his family were safe. Plus, as a cherry on top, God gave him a beautiful promise in the sky—a vibrant rainbow.

Abraham and Sarah Await Isaac (Genesis 12-21): When God first called Abram (later named Abraham), He promised not only to make him a great nation but also that through his offspring, all the nations of the earth would be blessed. However, this promise seemed impossible from a human perspective, as Abraham was 75 years old and Sarah was barren. Despite the improbability, Abraham chose to believe in God's promise, a decision credited to him as righteousness.

As years passed, the fulfillment of God's promise seemed increasingly remote. Sarah, growing impatient, offered her maidservant Hagar to Abraham, resulting in the birth of Ishmael. Yet, this was not the fulfillment of God's promise. When Abraham was 99 years old, God reaffirmed His covenant, specifically promising that Sarah would bear a son named Isaac. Sarah, overhearing this, laughed in disbelief due to her and Abraham's advanced age. Despite the laughter, the skepticism, and the decades of waiting, God's promise came to fruition when Sarah bore Isaac, embodying the joy and fulfillment of long-awaited promises.

The story of Abraham and Sarah waiting for Isaac teaches us lessons on the virtue of patience and the importance of faith in God's timing and promises. It demonstrates that even when circumstances seem utterly contrary to the fulfillment of a promise, God's plans are not bound by human limitations or expectations. Abraham's and Sarah's journey from doubt to fulfillment illustrates the transformative power of faith and patience, encouraging believers to trust in God's timing, even when it stretches far beyond our own understanding or expectations.

So, whenever you feel impatient or think that things are taking too long, remember Noah with his ark and Abraham and Sarah with their long-awaited son. Their stories remind us that with trust, patience, and a sprinkle of faith, we're all on a journey to something wonderful. Keep that chin up and keep on waiting; good things are on the horizon!

The benefits of being patient

You know, sometimes waiting can feel like the hardest thing, especially when you're super excited about something. As mentioned before, patience is like having a secret superpower. Here's why:

1. **Growth and Maturity:** Imagine a tiny caterpillar all wrapped up in its cocoon. It doesn't just pop out as a butterfly overnight. It takes time, waiting, and lots of transformation inside that cocoon. Similarly, when we patiently wait, we're also transforming. Those moments when we feel like nothing's happening. We're actually learning, growing, and getting stronger, just like that caterpillar. So, the next time you're waiting for something, think of it as your "cocoon time" - a special time to grow and get ready to spread your wings.

2. **Understanding and Empathy:** Have you ever noticed when someone lets you finish your story, even when you're speaking slowly or searching for words? That's them being patient. And it feels good, right? When

we're patient with others, we show them that we care about how they feel. It helps us really "walk in their shoes" and understand what they're going through. So, by being patient, not only are you being a rockstar listener, but you're also becoming a kinder and more caring friend.

3. **Reduced Stress:** Imagine you're trying to build the tallest tower with your blocks, but it keeps falling. If you rush and get frustrated, it feels stressful, right? But when you take a deep breath, stay patient, and try again calmly, it's way more fun! Being patient helps keep the stormy clouds of stress away, leaving you with a sunny, peaceful day.

So, the next time you find yourself tapping your feet or feeling restless, just remember that patience is your superpower. It helps you grow, understand others, and keep you calm and happy. Keep rocking that patience cape, and watch how it makes you and everyone around you smile!

Being Patient Every Day

In our daily lives, there are countless opportunities to practice patience.

You know, Jesus has this amazing way of showing patience to all of us. Wouldn't it be cool if we could show patience just like Him? Here are three ways you can do just that with your friends:

1. **Wait Your Turn:** You know how sometimes you're so eager to go on the swing or slide during recess? Well, just like Jesus waits for us, even when we take a little while to understand things, you can do the same. Next time you're at the playground, and everyone wants a turn, try saying, "Hey, you can go first. I'll wait." Trust me, waiting can be a game-changer and makes playtime fun for everyone.

2. **Listen Up:** Jesus is the best listener ever. He hears all our stories, big or small. So, when one of your friends is super excited to share something with you, give them your full attention. Even if their story is long or they're taking time to find the right words, stay with them. Show them you care by nodding, asking questions, or just being there. It's like giving them a mini-hug with your ears!

3. **Lend a Hand:** You're smart and super talented! But sometimes, just like all of us, your friends might need a bit of help. Jesus is always there to guide us, and you can do the same for your buddies. If you see someone stuck on a math problem or confused about something in class, offer to help. You could say, "Wanna see how I figured it out?" By sharing what you know, you're not just being patient, but you're also being a rockstar friend. (however, this would not be appropriate when

you are taking a test! ;o})

Remember, every time you show patience, it's like you're shining a little light, making the world a brighter place. You've got this!

Techniques for waiting nicely

1. **Deep Breathing**: When waiting gets tough, take a deep breath. Inhale slowly and exhale even slower. It'll calm your mind and body.

2. **Distraction**: If waiting is making you restless, divert your attention to something else. Maybe count the number of blue items in the room or sing a song in your mind.

3. **Positive Self-talk**: Remind yourself of the rewards of being patient. Think to yourself, "I can wait a bit longer, and it'll be worth it."

Praising moments of patience

Whenever you or someone around you displays patience, please take a moment to praise it. It can be as simple as saying, "I appreciate you for waiting so calmly," or "Thank you for being so patient." Such positive reinforcement will encourage even more patient behaviors in the future.

In conclusion, patience is a beautiful virtue that offers us growth, understanding, and peace. As we journey through life, remember that sometimes the best things come to those who wait. Just like after a rainy day, with a little patience, we can always look forward to a beautiful rainbow.

Chapter 5: Kindness

"Therefore, as God's chosen people, holy and dearly loved, clothe yourselves with compassion, kindness, humility, gentleness and patience." - Colossians 3:12

Uncovering Kindness

Kindness. It's a simple word, but it has a profound impact. At the heart of it, kindness means genuinely caring for others, wanting the best for them, and taking action to make a positive difference in their lives. It's like planting a seed of love wherever you go, knowing that each small act can grow into something beautiful.

Acts that show kindness

There are countless ways to show kindness, from a simple smile to a neighbor, to helping someone in need. Think of those times when you shared your snack with a friend who forgot theirs or when you cheered up a sibling who was feeling down. Those are all acts of kindness. The great thing about kindness is that it doesn't have to be big to be meaningful. Sometimes, the smallest gestures have the most significant impact.

Bible stories of compassion and care

The Bible is filled with stories of kindness and compassion.

The Widow's Offering (Mark 12:41-44): In the Gospel of Mark, the story of the widow's offering unfolds as Jesus sits opposite the temple treasury, observing people putting money into the offering box. Many rich individuals contribute large sums, making a show of their generosity. Amidst this, a poor widow approaches quietly and deposits two small copper coins, which together are worth only a fraction of a penny. This act might have gone unnoticed by most, given the modesty of the amount and the humble status of the woman, but it captures Jesus' attention.

Jesus calls his disciples to him and points out the widow's act as an extraordinary example of true giving. He explains that while the wealthy gave out of their abundance, contributing only a small portion of their surplus wealth, the widow, in her poverty, has given everything she had to live on. Her contribution, though financially minimal, is of immense value in the eyes of Jesus because it represents a profound act of faith, trust, and self-sacrifice. This story highlights the principle that the value of a gift is not measured by its size but by the spirit in which it is given. The widow's offering serves as a powerful lesson on the true nature of generosity and kindness, emphasizing the importance of the heart's intention over the magnitude of the gift.

The Feeding of the 5,000 (John 6:1-14): The Feeding of the 5,000 is one of the most well-known miracles of Jesus, recorded in all four Gospels, with the account in John providing specific details that highlight the theme of kindness and compassion. In this story, a large crowd has followed Jesus to a remote place because of the signs he was performing on the sick. As the day wears on, Jesus sees the multitude and, moved by compassion, recognizes their need for food. Instead of sending them away hungry, Jesus decides to feed them. He inquires about available food, and the disciples bring forward a young boy who has five barley loaves and two small fish. While this seems insufficient for such a large crowd, Jesus takes the loaves and fish, gives thanks, and distributes them to the people.

The act of feeding the 5,000 goes beyond merely satisfying physical hunger; it is a powerful demonstration of Jesus' kindness and concern for the well-being of the people. The miracle reveals Jesus' power over nature and His ability to provide abundantly for the needs of His followers. Furthermore, the involvement of the young boy with his modest offering underscores the theme that no act of kindness or contribution is too small in the hands of Jesus. It can be transformed and multiplied to achieve great things. This story teaches that kindness, coupled with faith, can lead to extraordinary outcomes, encouraging believers to trust in God's provision and to share what they have, no matter how little it might seem, to meet the needs of others.

Jesus Heals the Leper (Mark 1:40-45): In the narrative of Jesus healing the leper found in Mark, a leper approaches Jesus with a plea for cleansing, fully confident in Jesus' ability to heal him if He is willing. Leprosy at the time was not just a physical ailment but a condition that rendered individuals ritually unclean and socially ostracized, forcing them to live apart from the community and announce their impurity. Jesus moved with compassion, does something remarkable and culturally shocking: He reaches out and touches the man. This act alone was significant, as touching a leper would make one ritually unclean according to Jewish law. However, Jesus' touch conveys acceptance, dignity, and healing. He affirms His willingness to heal the man, saying, "I am willing; be clean," and immediately, the leprosy leaves the man.

This story goes beyond the physical healing of a dreadful disease; it illustrates a profound act of kindness that challenges social norms and stigma. Jesus' willingness to touch the leper breaks down the barriers of fear and prejudice, showcasing a model of inclusivity and compassion. The healing restores not only the man's physical health but also his social and relational standing, enabling him to rejoin the community and reconnect with those from whom he had been estranged. This act of kindness by Jesus emphasizes the value of every individual, regardless of their social status or condition, and teaches the transformative power of compassion and the importance of reaching out to those marginalized by society.

How Jesus was kind to everyone

Jesus, our ultimate role model, showcased kindness at every turn. He healed the sick, dined with those whom society had cast aside, and consistently put others before Himself. His actions were driven by pure love and compassion, making Him the epitome of kindness. The way He treated children, the stories He shared, and His ultimate sacrifice for us all are enduring examples of His boundless kindness.

Being Kind Every Day - Talking about kind acts we've seen or done

Discussing acts of kindness reinforces their importance. Maybe you saw someone help an elderly person cross the road or witnessed a friend stand up against bullying. Sharing these stories allows us to appreciate and learn from them. Kindness isn't a one-time act; it's a lifestyle. It's choosing to be gentle, understanding, and caring every day, in every situation.

Helping out at home

Simple acts like setting the table, assisting with chores, or making a bed can be acts of kindness towards your family. It shows respect and love for those you live with.

Being nice to classmates

School offers numerous opportunities for kindness. Sharing study notes, including someone in a game, or simply offering a listening ear when a classmate is upset can create a more loving environment.

Random acts of kindness ideas

1. Leaving Notes: Write kind note cards and leave them in library books for others to find.

2. Donating Old Toys: Give away toys you no longer play with to those in need.

3. Nature Cleanup: Spend an afternoon picking up litter in a park.

4. Baking for Neighbors: Bake some cookies and share them with neighbors just to make them smile.

In conclusion, kindness is a gift everyone can afford to give. It doesn't cost a thing but has immeasurable value. As we journey through life, let's remember that the world becomes a better place with each act of kindness. Whether we're sharing, caring, or simply being there for someone, our acts of kindness create ripples of love and positivity. And just as rain nourishes the earth, our kindness can nurture the souls of those around us.

Chapter 6: Goodness

"Do not be overcome by evil, but overcome evil with good." - Romans 12:21

Exploring Goodness

In a world filled with choices, standing firmly by what is right and good can sometimes feel like a challenge. From the playground to home, from school to the neighborhood, every day we're presented with numerous decisions. The quality of 'goodness' is all about choosing actions that reflect a good heart, even when no one is watching.

What does it mean to be good?

At first glance, 'being good' might sound like simply following rules or doing what you're told. But in truth, goodness goes much deeper. It's about the intentions of our hearts and the impact of our actions. To be good means to act with compassion, fairness, and honesty, especially in situations when it would be easier not to.

Bible examples of choosing the right path

The Good Samaritan (Luke 10:25-37): It begins with a lawyer testing Jesus, asking what he must do to inherit eternal life. Jesus responds with the question back to the lawyer, who answers with the commandment to love God and one's neighbor as oneself. Seeking to justify himself, the lawyer then asks, "And who is my neighbor?" In response, Jesus tells the story of The Good Samaritan.

The story unfolds with a man traveling from Jerusalem to Jericho who is attacked by robbers, beaten, stripped, and left half-dead by the roadside. A priest and then a Levite, both respected figures in Jewish society, pass by the injured man, choosing to avoid him and continue on their way. In contrast, a Samaritan, considered an outcast and enemy by the Jews of the time, stops to help the injured man. He bandages his wounds, transports him on his own animal to an inn, and pays for his care, promising to cover any additional expenses upon his return.

The parable of The Good Samaritan teaches just how big the term "neighbor" really is. It emphasizes that kindness and compassion should extend beyond the limits of social, ethnic, or religious boundaries. The Samaritan's actions embody the essence of true neighborly love and the principle of treating others as one would wish to be treated, regardless of their background or status. This story challenges us to show mercy and act with goodness towards all people, illustrating that the practice of genuine compassion is a fundamental aspect of living a life aligned with God's will.

David and Mephibosheth (2 Samuel 9): The story of David and Mephibosheth presents a moving example of kindness, loyalty, and the restoration of dignity to the less fortunate. Mephibosheth was the son of Jonathan and the grandson of Saul, the king of Israel before David. After Saul and Jonathan were killed in battle, Mephibosheth, then a young child, was crippled in both feet during an accident that occurred as his nurse fled with him in panic.

Years later, King David, remembering his covenant of friendship with Jonathan, sought out any remaining members of Saul's family to show them kindness. He discovered Mephibosheth, who was living in obscurity and likely expecting retribution, as was customary when new dynasties took power. Instead of seeking revenge, David restored to Mephibosheth all the lands that had belonged to Saul and invited him to eat regularly at the king's table, effectively treating him as one of his own sons.

This story illustrates several important themes. Firstly, it underscores the value of kindness and loyalty that transcend familial and political boundaries. David's actions towards Mephibosheth demonstrate a commitment to honor his promise to Jonathan, showing that true friendship and loyalty outlive even death. Secondly, the narrative highlights the theme of restoration and grace. Despite Mephibosheth's lineage and his disability, David restores his fortune and dignity, integrating him into the royal household. This act of generosity reflects the broader biblical themes of redemption and the inclusive nature of God's kingdom, where mercy and kindness are extended to all, irrespective of their past or their physical condition.

Dorcas' Acts of Kindness (Acts 9:36-42): Dorcas was a disciple who lived in Joppa, and she was well-known for her good deeds and acts of charity, particularly for making clothes for the widows and the needy in her community. Her life was a testament to her faith, expressed through her selfless service to others.

Tragically, Dorcas fell ill and died, leaving the community in mourning. Her body was washed and placed in an upper room. When the disciples heard that Peter was nearby in Lydda, they sent two men to urgently request his presence, hoping for a miracle. Upon his arrival, Peter was taken to the room where Dorcas' body lay, surrounded by grieving widows who showed him the tunics and garments Dorcas had made for them. Peter sent everyone out of the room, knelt down to pray, and then, turning to her body, said, "Tabitha, get up." Miraculously, she opened her eyes, saw Peter, and sat up. He took her by the hand, helped her to her feet, and presented her alive to the saints and widows. The news of this miracle spread throughout Joppa, leading many to believe in the Lord.

The story of Dorcas highlights the profound impact of kindness and charitable acts in a community. Dorcas' legacy was not just in the clothes she made but in the love and care she poured into her community, embodying the Christian call to serve and love one another. Her resurrection by God through Peter not only underscores the power of God working through the apostles but also serves to amplify the importance of Dorcas' life and deeds. Her story teaches children and adults alike the value of compassion and generosity, illustrating that acts of goodness can leave a lasting imprint on the hearts of those around us and, in some cases, can lead to extraordinary outcomes that reaffirm faith and inspire entire communities.

Times when it's tough to be good

It's not always easy to be good. Peer pressure, wanting to fit in, or even just a tempting situation can sometimes make it challenging to choose the right path. Remembering the story of Joseph and his brothers can be helpful here. Even when sold into slavery by his siblings, Joseph maintained his integrity and trusted in God. Eventually, he rose to great power and was in a position to save his family during a famine. His journey wasn't easy, but he always leaned towards goodness.

Goodness Through Play

Believe it or not, playtime can be a brilliant way to understand and explore the concept of goodness. Playtime isn't just about having fun; it's like a colorful, open book that teaches us so many things without us even realizing it. And one of those things is goodness. Yes, you heard that right! Through play, we can learn and show what it means to be good, just like the heroes in those Bible stories.

1. **Team Games and Sportsmanship:** When you're playing a team game, whether it's soccer, basketball, or even a board game, there's a golden opportunity to practice goodness. Being a good sport means playing fair, following the rules, and respecting everyone - even the other team. It's not just about winning; it's about how you play the game. Cheering for your teammates, giving a high five to the opposing team, or even helping someone up when they fall – that's showing goodness in action.

2. **Sharing and Taking Turns:** Whether you're at the park or in your backyard, sharing your toys or taking turns on the swing demonstrates goodness. It's like saying, "I care about your happiness as much as mine." This simple act of sharing brings smiles and spreads joy, just like the warmth and forgiveness in the story of the Prodigal Son.

3. **Role-Playing Games:** Ever pretended to be a superhero, a teacher, or maybe a doctor? Role-playing games are amazing for sparking imagination, but they also let you walk in someone else's shoes for a bit. This helps you understand others better, showing empathy and compassion, which are big parts of being good. You learn to solve problems, help others, and make fair de-

cisions in your imaginative play world.

4. **Building and Creating Together:** When you build something with someone else, like a giant LEGO castle or a cool sandcastle, you're working together, sharing ideas, and respecting each other's creativity. It teaches you that by cooperating and being kind, you can create something beautiful and have lots of fun doing it!

So, you see, playtime is like a mini-world where you can practice being good in so many ways. Each game, each shared laugh, and every high five is a step towards understanding what goodness truly means. And just like Daniel, Joseph, and the father of the Prodigal Son, you learn that goodness might not always be the easiest path, but it's definitely the most rewarding and fun one when you're playing!

The Power of Sharing Good Choices:

Sharing our moments of goodness is not just about recounting our good deeds; it's about building a foundation of moral understanding and empathy. When we take the time to sit together and share the instances when we chose the path of goodness, it becomes an enriching experience for everyone involved.

Imagine this: your family is gathered around, maybe after dinner or during a weekend hangout, and you start to share stories. Not just any stories, but personal anecdotes about times when you were faced with a choice and opted for goodness. These stories don't have to be grand or dramatic; even the simplest acts of kindness, fairness, and honesty shine brightly.

For others, hearing about the time you returned a lost wallet, stood up for a friend, or even chose to be patient in a frustrating situation, is incredibly impactful. It shows them that goodness isn't just a concept in fairy tales or ancient stories; it's alive and thriving in the everyday actions of the people they know and look up to.

Reflection and Discussion:

This sharing session becomes a treasure trove of life lessons. But it's not just about listening; it's also about engaging. Ask others what they think about each story shared. Would they have done the same? What would they have found difficult? This isn't about judging choices but understanding the layers of thought and emotion behind each act of goodness.

Balancing the Narrative:

And here's something equally important: discussing the times we've stumbled. Yes, everyone makes mistakes or faces moments of weakness. Sharing these moments with the same openness as the good choices is crucial. It lets others know that it's okay to not always get it right, as long as we learn, grow, and strive to do better next time.

This balanced narrative helps us understand that the journey of goodness is ongoing. It's not about being perfect but about continually choosing to act with compassion, fairness, and integrity, even when it's challenging.

Celebrating Goodness:

Finally, let's celebrate these moments of goodness, no matter how small. Recognition and appreciation go a long way in reinforcing and developing positive behavior. It's a gentle reminder that goodness is valued, celebrated, and an integral part of who we are as a family.

By sharing and discussing our good choices, we not only highlight the beauty of doing right by others but also instill a deep-seated sense of morality and empathy.

Reflecting on our choices

At the end of each day, taking a moment to reflect on our actions can be incredibly beneficial. It's an opportunity to consider the choices made, appreciate the good ones, and think about how to improve on any not-so-great decisions.

In conclusion, goodness is a path that might sometimes be challenging but is always rewarding. It's a journey of the heart, one where every step, every choice, molds us into better versions of ourselves. In the end, choosing good over bad isn't just about doing the right thing; it's about shaping a world filled with love, compassion, and goodness.

Chapter 7: Faithfulness

"Let love and faithfulness never leave you; bind them around your neck, write them on the tablet of your heart." - Proverbs 3:3

Discovering Faithfulness

Imagine your favorite blanket - the one that keeps you warm, snug, and feels oh-so-comfortable. No matter how many times you've used it, it always remains the same: cozy and reliable. That's a bit like faithfulness. Faithfulness is all about being dependable, trustworthy, and steadfast. When someone is faithful, you can count on them no matter what.

Loyalty and Trust in the Bible

The Story of Abraham's Test Genesis 22:1-13

The Bible is full of examples that shine a light on loyalty and trust. Abraham is one of my favorite Old Testament examples. Abraham wasn't just any ordinary man; he was a friend of God, known for his unwavering faith and trust in God. But one day, Abraham faced the greatest test of his life, a test that would show just how deep his trust in God really was.

God had blessed Abraham with a son named Isaac. Isaac was not just a son to Abraham; he was a precious gift, especially because Abraham and his wife, Sarah, had waited many, many years for him. Abraham loved Isaac more than anything in the world.

Then, one day, God asked Abraham to do something that seemed beyond understanding. God wanted Abraham to take Isaac to a mountain and offer him as a sacrifice. Now, to us, this request might seem confusing and even scary. But back in those times, such tests were ways to show deep trust and faithfulness.

Abraham was faced with a choice that would make anyone's heart ache. Imagine being asked to give up something or someone you love dearly. It's not easy, right? But Abraham, even with his heart heavy, chose to trust God completely. He believed that God's plans were good, even if they didn't make sense to him.

So, Abraham and Isaac set off on a journey to the mountain that God had told them about. Isaac, who was a smart and observant boy, noticed that they were carrying everything needed for a sacrifice, like wood and fire, but there was no lamb to offer.

"Father," Isaac asked, "where is the lamb for the burnt offering?"

Abraham replied with gentle assurance, "God Himself will provide the lamb for the burnt offering, my son." Abraham's words were a beacon of faith, shining with trust in God's goodness.

When they reached the place God had told him about, Abraham built an altar and arranged the wood on it. As Abraham prepared to follow through with God's difficult request, his heart was undoubtedly racing, his mind swirling with thoughts, yet his trust in God never wavered.

But just as Abraham was about to make the ultimate sacrifice, an angel called out to him from heaven, "Abraham! Abraham!"

"Here I am," he replied.

The angel said, "Do not lay a hand on the boy. Do not do anything to him. Now I know that you fear God because you have not withheld from me your son, your only son."

At that moment, Abraham looked up and saw a ram caught by its horns in a thicket. He understood that God had provided a sacrifice. The ram was offered in Isaac's place, and Isaac was safe. This moment was a powerful reminder of Abraham's faith and trust in God.

Through this story, we learn that faithfulness means trusting God, even when His plans seem mysterious or challenging. Abraham's trust in God was rewarded, and as promised, he became the father of many nations. His descendants were as numerous as the stars in the sky he once gazed upon, a beautiful testament to the strength of faithfulness and trust.

So, whenever we're faced with tough situations or decisions that don't make sense, let's remember Abraham's story. Let's be brave like Abraham, holding onto our trust in God, believing in

His promises, and knowing that He always has a plan for us, just as He did for Abraham and Isaac.

The Story of Ruth -Ruth 1-4

Ruth's story is one of true loyalty and faithfulness. Ruth was married to Naomi's son, but tragedy struck when Naomi lost not only her husband but both of her sons as well, including Ruth's husband. In those times, for a woman to lose her husband and sons meant more than just losing loved ones; it meant losing her security and place in society.

Naomi, heartbroken and defeated, decided to return to her homeland of Bethlehem. She urged her daughters-in-law, Ruth and Orpah, to stay in Moab and remarry, as she had nothing left to offer them. Orpah, tearfully, decided to stay behind, but Ruth's response was different.

With a heart full of love and determination, Ruth spoke words that would echo through the ages, "Where you go, I will go, and where you stay, I will stay. Your people will be my people and your God my God." These weren't just words; they were a solemn vow, a commitment that Ruth made not only to Naomi but to God as well.

So, Ruth left everything she knew behind—her family, her land, her people—to accompany Naomi to Bethlehem. Imagine how difficult that must have been. Ruth stepped into a world unknown, with only her faithfulness to guide her.

In Bethlehem, Ruth faced the reality of her and Naomi's situation. They needed food and support, so Ruth took it upon herself to work and provide for them both. She went to the fields to glean leftover grains, a practice allowed for the poor and the widows. The field she happened to work in belonged to a man named Boaz, who was not only wealthy but also a relative of Naomi's late husband.

Boaz noticed Ruth from the very start, not just because of her hard work but also because of the loyalty and kindness she showed Naomi. Word of Ruth's faithfulness had spread, and Boaz was moved by her dedication. He ensured that Ruth was protected in his fields and had enough to glean, showing favor towards her.

Ruth's unwavering dedication to Naomi led not only to their survival but to a new beginning. Boaz, struck by Ruth's loyalty and character, took her as his wife. This union blessed Naomi with a family once again and Ruth with a new, secure life. Moreover, Ruth and Boaz's lineage would become one of great significance, leading to King David and, eventually, to Jesus Christ himself.

Ruth's story teaches us that faithfulness isn't just about sticking by someone in easy times; it's about holding on and walking together through the storms of life. It's about making sacrifices for the sake of others and trusting that God has a plan through it all.

So, whenever we face tough choices or when loyalty is tested, let's remember Ruth. Let's remember that sometimes, faithfulness means taking the harder road, not for our gain but for the love and care of others. And in this journey, we're never alone; just as Ruth had Naomi and Boaz came to support Ruth, God is with us, guiding our steps toward a future filled with hope and blessing.

The Story of Shadrach, Meshach, and Abednego Daniel 3

These three were not just ordinary young men; they were captives from Judah, living in Babylon, yet they had risen to positions of trust because of their wisdom and integrity. However, their greatest challenge was yet to come, a challenge that would test their faithfulness to the utmost.

King Nebuchadnezzar, in his pride, made a colossal golden statue and decreed that everyone must bow down and worship this image when music played. The penalty for defying this order was a terrifying one: to be thrown into a blazing furnace. The king's command put everyone in the kingdom to the test, but for Shadrach, Meshach, and Abednego, the choice was clear.

Their faith in God was unwavering, their principles unshakeable. They knew they could not bow to any god but the one true God they worshiped. When the music sounded, signaling the time to bow, everyone in the kingdom fell to their knees except for these three courageous young men.

Word of their defiance reached the king, and in his fury, he summoned them. Nebuchadnezzar, in disbelief, offered them one more chance to bow down to his golden statue. But Shadrach, Meshach, and Abednego remained resolute. They responded to the king with words that echoed their unbreakable faith, "O Nebuchadnezzar, we do not need to defend ourselves before you in this matter. If we are thrown into the blazing furnace, the God we serve is able to save us from it, and He will rescue us from your hand, O king. But even if He does not, we want you to know, O king, that we will not serve your gods or worship the image of gold you have set up."

Enraged, King Nebuchadnezzar ordered the furnace to be heated seven times hotter than usual. The flames were so intense that the soldiers who threw Shadrach, Meshach, and Abednego into the furnace were consumed by the fire. But when the king looked into the furnace, his anger turned to astonishment. Instead of three men consumed by the flames, he saw four men walking unharmed in the fire, and the fourth looked like "the Son of God."

Realizing the miraculous nature of their deliverance, Nebuchadnezzar called them out of the furnace. To everyone's amazement, not a hair on their heads was singed, their clothes were unharmed, and they didn't even smell of smoke. This miraculous event showed not only their faithfulness but the power and faithfulness of their God.

The courage and trust of Shadrach, Meshach, and Abednego led to a remarkable outcome. King Nebuchadnezzar, who had once ordered everyone to worship his golden image, now praised their God, proclaiming, "Praise be to the God of Shadrach, Meshach, and Abednego, who has sent his angel and rescued his servants! They trusted in him and defied the king's command and were willing to give up their lives rather than serve or worship any god except their own God."

Furthermore, the king made a decree that no one, anywhere, should speak against the God of Shadrach, Meshach, and Abednego, acknowledging the might and sovereignty of their God.

This story of Shadrach, Meshach, and Abednego teaches us about the power of steadfast faith and the importance of being faithful to our beliefs in God, even in the face of the fiercest trials. Their story is a testament to the fact that when we stand firm in our faith, trusting in God's plans and protection, extraordinary things can happen, not only for us but also influencing those around us, just as it did with King Nebuchadnezzar.

How Being Faithful Helps Us

Have you ever had a friend who you could trust with anything? The kind of friend who would be there when you needed them, and never let you down? That's the beauty of faithfulness. Being a faithful friend ensures stronger bonds and deeper connections. When we're reliable, it builds trust, and this trust serves as the foundation for lasting relationships.

Faithfulness teaches us resilience and commitment, qualities that deepen our relationships. It's like planting a tree; the more we nurture it with trust and reliability, the deeper its roots grow, making it unshakable even in the fiercest winds. This staying power in friendship not only strengthens our bonds but also shapes us into more dependable, compassionate individuals, creating a ripple effect that enriches our entire community.

Being Loyal Every Day

Every day presents opportunities to practice faithfulness. Whether it's by keeping a promise, being there for a friend, or simply being honest, everyday acts of loyalty can have a lasting impact. Incorporating faithfulness into our daily routines might seem small, like holding the door open for someone or remembering to call a friend who's going through a tough time, but these acts of kindness echo the depth of our loyalty.

Over time, these consistent gestures build a picture of trust, showing those around us that we value integrity and commitment. It's in these moments, often unnoticed, where the true essence of loyalty shines brightest, transforming ordinary days into a testament of our steadfastness and love.

Trust Exercises with Friends

Building trust is a vital aspect of any relationship. Try these simple exercises, like blindfolded obstacle courses where one friend guides another or two-person artwork where one describes and the other draws. It will not only be fun, but it will help you see how trust plays a vital role in friendships. If you really think about it, you wouldn't want to do this with someone who you didn't trust. You trust the person who has been a faithful friend.

Keeping Promises

Promises are not just words; they're commitments. Whenever we make a promise, whether it's to finish our homework or help out with chores, it's essential to follow through. By doing so, we show that we're reliable and trustworthy.

In conclusion, faithfulness is a beautiful and essential fruit of the spirit. In a world that's constantly changing, being someone that others can rely on is invaluable. Whether it's through stories, songs, games, or everyday acts, cultivating and celebrating faithfulness enriches our lives and the lives of those around us.

Chapter 8: Gentleness

"Let your gentleness be evident to all. The Lord is near." - Philippians 4:5

Embracing Gentleness

Imagine a butterfly landing on a delicate flower, or the soft rustle of leaves in a gentle breeze. There's a beauty and strength in such softness and delicacy. In life, there are moments that call for power and might, but there are many more instances where gentleness and kindness shine the brightest.

Understanding the Strength in Softness

Being gentle doesn't mean being weak. Think about water – it's soft and flowing, but over time, it can shape mountains and carve valleys. In the same way, a gentle heart can make a significant impact on the world around us. It's the strength to respond with softness even when faced with challenges, and it's choosing kindness over anger.

Bible Stories about Handling Situations Gently

The Bible gives us many examples of gentleness in action.

Jesus and the woman caught in adultery (John 8:1-11)

This testimony is a profound example of gentleness in the face of potential condemnation. The narrative begins with Jesus teaching in the temple when the scribes and Pharisees bring before Him a woman caught in the act of adultery, a crime punishable by stoning according to Mosaic Law. They question Jesus, attempting to trap Him into saying something they could use against Him. If Jesus were to dismiss the charges, He would appear to condone sin, but if He urged them to execute her, He would be in conflict with Roman law, which reserved capital punishment for itself.

Instead of reacting impulsively or harshly, Jesus responds with remarkable gentleness and wisdom. He stoops down and writes in the dirt with His finger, not immediately addressing their question. As they continue to press Him, He stands and delivers the famous line, "Let any one of you who is without sin be the first to throw a stone at her." One by one, beginning with the oldest, the accusers leave until only Jesus and the woman remain. Jesus then stands up again, and seeing no one but the woman, He asks her where her accusers have gone and if no one has condemned her. When she replies that no one has, Jesus responds with gentle grace, "Neither do I condemn you; go now and leave your life of sin."

This story highlights the power of gentleness and compassion over judgment and condemnation. Jesus defuses a volatile situation with calmness and wisdom, protecting the woman's life and offering her a chance for redemption. The narrative teaches that while sin is to be acknowledged, the approach to dealing with it should be characterized by understanding and the opportunity for repentance, rather than harsh judgment. Jesus exemplifies a gentle response that preserves dignity and encourages transformation, reminding us of the importance of compassion and forgiveness in our interactions with others, especially when they are at their most vulnerable.

David Spares Saul's Life (1 Samuel 24): The story of David sparing Saul's life unfolds as a dramatic encounter between the future king of Israel and the reigning monarch. Saul, consumed by jealousy and fear of David's rising popularity and God's favor towards him, sets out to kill David. David, along with his men, finds refuge in the caves of En Gedi. Unbeknownst to Saul, while he enters one of these caves to relieve himself, David and his men are hiding deeper within the same cave.

In this vulnerable moment for Saul, David's men see an opportunity for David to kill Saul, interpreting the situation as God delivering Saul into David's hands. However, David chooses a path of remarkable restraint and gentleness. Instead of killing Saul, he secretly cuts off a corner of Saul's robe. Even this act causes David to feel remorseful for having "cut off a corner of [the king's] robe" as he respects Saul's anointed status by God. After Saul leaves the cave, David emerges to reveal his action, demonstrating to Saul that he had the opportunity to kill him but chose not to. David's words and actions convey a message of respect, loyalty, and the refusal to harm the Lord's anointed, despite Saul's intentions against him.

This story is a powerful testament to the strength inherent in gentleness and the choice of mercy over vengeance. David's decision to spare Saul's life, even when it seemed justifiable to take revenge, showcases the virtue of respecting God's plan and the dignity of every individual, even one's enemies. It highlights the principle that true leadership and honor are rooted in the ability to respond with gentleness and integrity, even in the face of aggression and hostility. Through this act of mercy, David not only preserves his moral integrity but also sets an example for his men and for future generations about the power of a gentle spirit over might or vengeance.

Joseph Reassures His Brothers (Genesis 50:15-21): After the death of their father Jacob, Joseph's brothers feared retribution for their past actions of selling Joseph into slavery. They were concerned that Joseph had been restraining his vengeance out of respect for their father and that, with Jacob gone, Joseph might now seek revenge. In their anxiety, they sent a message to Joseph, claiming it was their father's wish for Joseph to forgive his brothers. When they met, the brothers even offered themselves as slaves to Joseph, demonstrating their guilt and fear of possible retaliation.

Joseph's response to his brothers was one of profound gentleness and compassion. He was moved to tears by their plea and reassured them that he had no intention of harming them. Joseph told his brothers not to be afraid, for he was not in the place of God to exact vengeance. He acknowledged the evil of their actions but chose to focus on the positive outcome, stating that God had used their deeds to save many lives during the famine. Instead of seeking vengeance, Joseph promised to provide for them and their children, ensuring their safety and well-being.

This story exemplifies the power of gentleness and forgiveness. Joseph's gentle reassurance to his brothers not only calmed their fears but also healed a family torn apart by jealousy and wrong-doing. It highlights the importance of seeing beyond personal hurt to the broader picture of God's plan and the potential for good even in adverse circumstances. Joseph's actions teach that gentleness, forgiveness, and trust in God's sovereignty can transform relationships and bring about healing and reconciliation.

The Grace of Being Kind and Soft

Being gentle means treating others the way you'd want to be treated. It's realizing that every person has feelings and that our actions and words can impact them deeply. Jesus embodied this throughout his life, teaching his followers the value of being meek and gentle-hearted.

Being Gentle Every Day

Life is filled with moments that test our patience and gentleness. But each day also brings countless opportunities to showcase our gentleness, both in action and words.

Handling Things with Care

For instance, consider the way we treat a pet. Pets are living creatures that rely on us for care and affection. We use gentle hands to pet them, careful not to be too rough, which shows our respect and love for them. Just like pets, other things in our world need to be treated with kindness and care too.

Think about the simple act of turning the pages of a book. Books are gateways to adventure, learning, and imagination, but they are also delicate objects that can be damaged if we're not careful. By turning the pages gently, we show respect for the stories and knowledge held within, and we ensure that others can enjoy the book after us. This same idea applies to toys, belongings, and even the environment—like picking up a flower or handling a bug. When we treat everything around us with gentleness, we're not only taking care of our things and nature, but we're also learning an important value: respect. This respect for our belongings, for others, and for the world around us helps make the world a kinder, gentler place for everyone to live in.

Speaking Softly and Kindly

Words have power, and the way we use them can make a big difference. A gentle word can calm a crying friend, and a soft voice can soothe a scared heart. When I was growing up, there was an old saying, "If you don't have anything nice to say, don't say anything at all." We need to encourage one another to use our words for comfort, praise, and kindness so that we can cultivate a lifetime of gentle speech.

In conclusion, gentleness is one of the most powerful qualities a person can possess. It's the choice to act with kindness, to speak with softness, and to handle everything with care. The world can sometimes be a challenging and noisy place, but with gentleness, we can bring a touch of calm and serenity to it. By embedding this quality into our hearts, we ensure a future filled with compassion, understanding, and grace.

Chapter 9:
Self-Control

"Like a city whose walls are broken through is a person who lacks self-control." - Proverbs 25:28

Learning Self-Control - Taming the Inner Wild Horse

Imagine a wild horse, galloping freely across the plains, its mane flowing with the wind, and nothing holding it back. While the sight is magnificent, a tamed horse can offer much to the community: it can carry heavy loads, help plow the fields, and even become a loyal companion. Just like the wild horse, our emotions and impulses can sometimes run free, but with self-control, we can harness them for better purposes.

Why it's sometimes hard to control ourselves

Each one of us has a range of feelings, from bubbling excitement to deep disappointment. These emotions can be quite powerful, pushing us to act without thinking. Maybe you've felt the urge to shout when you're upset, or perhaps you've wanted to grab a third piece of cake even though you're full. This is entirely natural! However, self-control is about recognizing these impulses and deciding how to act on them.

Bible Examples of Resisting Temptations

The Bible is rich with stories that teach us about the value of self-control.

Joseph Resists Temptation (Genesis 39): Joseph, sold into slavery by his brothers, finds himself in Egypt, serving in the household of Potiphar, an officer of Pharaoh. Joseph excels in his duties, earning Potiphar's trust and becoming overseer of his house. However, Potiphar's wife repeatedly attempts to tempt Joseph. Despite the potential benefits of yielding to her advances—possibly gaining favor or avoiding conflict—Joseph steadfastly refuses. He recognizes the moral and ethical implications, emphasizing that giving in would be a sin against God and a betrayal of Potiphar's trust. When she makes a final attempt, grabbing his cloak, Joseph flees, leaving his garment behind.

This moment leads to Joseph being falsely accused by Potiphar's wife, who presents the cloak as evidence of Joseph's supposed advances. Despite his innocence and the unjust consequences, Joseph is imprisoned. This story highlights Joseph's remarkable self-control and his commitment to righteousness, even in the face of severe temptation and subsequent hardship. Joseph's ability to prioritize his integrity and his faithfulness to God over immediate personal gain is a powerful lesson in the value of self-control. It teaches that true strength lies not in succumbing to momentary desires but in adhering to one's principles, even when the right choice leads to challenging outcomes. Joseph's story reassures us that maintaining integrity and trusting in God's plan despite unfair circumstances can lead to greater fulfillment and divine favor in the long run.

Jesus' Temptation in the Wilderness (Matthew 4:1-11): The story of Jesus' temptation in the wilderness unfolds immediately after Jesus' baptism, marking the beginning of His public ministry. Led by the Spirit into the desert, Jesus fasts for 40 days and nights, a period of preparation and spiritual fortitude. It is in this state of physical vulnerability that Satan approaches Him with a series of temptations, each designed to exploit human weakness and challenge Jesus' obedience to God's will.

The first temptation involves turning stones into bread, appealing to Jesus' physical hunger. The second temptation is to test God's protection by throwing Himself down from the temple's pinnacle, challenging the trust in divine care. The third and final temptation Satan offers Jesus is all the kingdoms of the world in exchange for worshiping him, targeting the desire for power and authority. In each case, Jesus responds with quotations from Scripture, not only resisting temptation but also affirming His complete reliance on God's word and authority. Jesus' refusals emphasize the principles of living by every word that comes from God, not testing God, and worshiping only the Lord.

This story highlights the importance of self-control and the power of God's word as a tool for resisting temptation. Jesus demonstrates that physical needs, pride, and the allure of power should not dictate our actions when they conflict with God's will. For children, this story serves as an example of using wisdom and self-control in difficult situations, and it underscores the importance of knowing and relying on God's word for guidance and strength in times of challenge.

Benefits of mastering our impulses

Imagine being able to handle disappointments without tears or facing a challenging task without giving up. Self-control equips us to manage our reactions, leading to better relationships, more accomplishments, and a greater sense of well-being. When we pause and think before we act, we make choices that are more in line with who we want to be.

Using Self-Control Every Day

Practicing self-control is like strengthening a muscle; the more we use it, the stronger it becomes. By incorporating techniques and reminders into our daily lives, we can enhance our ability to remain calm, thoughtful, and in control.

Techniques for managing excitement or disappointment

- **Deep Breathing:** Whenever feelings become too intense, take a moment to breathe deeply. Count to four while inhaling, hold for four counts, then exhale for another four counts.

- **Counting to Ten:** If something upsets you, before reacting, count to ten slowly. This gives you a chance to calm down and think about your response.

Creating a Self-Control Reward Chart

Create a chart with various self-control challenges, like "I spoke kindly even when I was upset" or "I waited patiently without complaining." Every time you accomplishes one of these challenges, you can place a sticker or draw a star on the chart. After a certain number of stickers or stars, you can receive a reward that you work out with your parents or caregiver. This visual representation can be motivating and make the journey of mastering self-control even more rewarding.

In conclusion, self-control is one of the most essential skills we can nurture when we are young. It prepares us to handle the ups and downs of life gracefully, make thoughtful decisions, and develop into responsible, mature individuals. Like taming the wild horse within, with patience and perseverance, we can harness our emotions and impulses, channeling them into positive actions that benefit not only ourselves but also those around us.

Conclusion: Becoming a Fruitful Explorer

"But the fruit of the Spirit is love, joy, peace, patience, kindness, goodness, faithfulness, gentleness, and self-control." - Galatians 5:22-23

Mixing the Fruits - Blending All the Fruits Together

Imagine a delicious fruit basket filled with a variety of colorful and tasty fruits. Each fruit has its unique flavor and texture, but when they are combined, they create a delightful and harmonious medley. Similarly, the Fruit of the Spirit, though distinct in their characteristics, come together to shape a complete and balanced Christian life. Each "fruit" enhances and complements the others, helping us develop a well-rounded character.

How all the Fruit of the Spirit work together

- **Love** provides the foundation, as it's the root from which all other virtues sprout. It motivates our actions and deepens our compassion.

- **Joy** and **Peace** nourish our inner well-being, ensuring we remain content and grounded.

- **Patience, Kindness,** and **Goodness** guide our interactions, ensuring we treat others with respect and understanding.

- **Faithfulness** strengthens our bond with God, while **Gentleness** and **Self-Control** teach us to approach situations with a calm and considerate demeanor.

All these virtues intertwine, helping us face life's challenges with grace and wisdom.

Bible characters who showed multiple fruits

- **Joseph** displayed **Patience** during his years in prison, **Faithfulness** to God's plan, and **Kindness** when he forgave his brothers.

- **Ruth** showcased her **Loyalty** and **Goodness** by staying with Naomi, her **Love** was evident in her commitment, and her **Joy** blossomed when she found a new family with Boaz.

- **Daniel** exhibited **Faithfulness** by praying to God despite the king's decree, **Self-Control** when he opted for vegetables over the king's feast, and **Peace** in the lion's den.

Each of these characters, through their trials and tribulations, demonstrated a blend of the Fruit of the Spirit, reminding us of the beauty of a pure spiritual life.

The beauty of a balanced spirit

Just as a balanced diet helps our physical health, a balanced spirit nurtures our soul. Embracing all the Fruit of the Spirit ensures we are not just kind but also patient, not just joyful but also peaceful. This biblical approach to spirituality enriches our relationship with God, with others, and with ourselves.

Celebrating All We've Learned

Our spiritual voyage through the Fruit of the Spirit is drawing to a close, and it's a heartwarming moment to reflect on the profound insights we've gathered. Each chapter, each lesson, has been a unique revelation, unveiling the essence of a life that mirrors God's boundless love and wisdom. Like the branches of a fruit-bearing tree, our understanding has grown, sprouted leaves, and now bears the sweet fruit of spiritual enlightenment.

Navigating the intricate realms of **Love, Joy, Peace, Patience, Kindness, Goodness, Faithfulness, Gentleness,** and **Self-Control**, we have journeyed across an expansive spiritual terrain. Let's recap the essence of these cherished learnings:

- **Love:** It manifested as an innate, unwavering affection, reminding us that true love flows unconditionally, demanding nothing in return.

- **Joy:** More than a fleeting emotion, it is a profound inner contentment anchored in our faith, revealing that genuine joy radiates even in trials.

- **Peace:** We recognized the tranquil depths of true peace, realizing it's not about the absence of turmoil but the presence of trust in God.

- **Patience:** This taught us that waiting is an act of hope, showcasing our trust in God's timing and the unfolding of His plans.

- Kindness & Goodness: We learned the power of benevolence, understanding that true goodness arises from a place of compassion and seeking the well-being of others.

- **Faithfulness:** It showcased unwavering loyalty, emphasizing the beauty of standing firm in our beliefs and commitments.

- **Gentleness:** Here, we grasped the might of softness, realizing that sometimes the most profound strength is displayed not in dominance but in understanding and kindness.

- **Self-Control:** We looked at the mastery of our impulses, recognizing the empowerment that comes from reigning in our desires and reactions.

Our metaphorical basket, brimming with these fruits, is now a testament to the transformative power of the scriptures and God's guiding hand.

The Lifelong Journey of the Fruit of the Spirit

While the pages of this book might end, the journey of growing in the knowledge of the Fruit of the Spirit is continual. Each day presents a lot of opportunities to live these virtues, to choose love over indifference, patience over haste, and gentleness over harshness.

Life will, of course, throw its challenges. We will encounter crossroads where our values will be tested. Yet, fortified with the wisdom of the Fruit of the Spirit, we possess the tools to navigate these situations with grace.

A tree doesn't bear fruit just once; it's a recurring miracle, reflecting the seasons of growth, nurturing, and eventual fruition. Similarly, our relationship with the Fruit of the Spirit is a continual journey nurtured by our experiences and choices.

Encouraging Continuous Growth and Exploration

Now, as we step out and truly walk in the fruit of the spirit, it's important to nurture this newfound wisdom. Here are some ways to continually grow in the light of the Fruit of the Spirit:

- **Daily Wonder Time:** Let's make some time every day to think quietly. Remember when you were super kind or patient today? And if there were times when you could have been a little nicer or more patient, that's okay too! It's all about learning and doing better next time.

- **Bible Adventure:** The Bible is like a treasure map, filled with stories and inspirations that can help us be our best selves. Whenever you're feeling puzzled or just want a boost of encouragement, open up your Bible and start exploring!

- **Chat and Share:** Talking with your family and friends about the cool things you're learning about kindness, patience, and all the other awesome ways we can act is really fun. It's like passing around a basket of goodies where everyone can take a piece and share one too!

- **High-Five Moments:** Whenever you notice someone being extra kind or patient, or maybe when you've done something really nice, give them(or yourself) a big high-five! It's like saying, "Hey, you're doing great!" and it makes everyone feel super special.

- Always Curious Club: Remember, even though we're learning a lot and getting really good at walking in love, joy, and the peace of God, as well as being patient, kind, good, faithful, gentle, and walking in self-control, there's always more to discover. Being curious and ready to learn more is what makes this adventure so exciting!

In wrapping up our "Adventures in Scriptures for Kids: Exploring the Fruit of the Spirit," remember that this isn't an end but a beginning. We are now ambassadors of these God-given virtues, entrusted with the mission to make our surroundings a little more loving, a tad more peaceful, and significantly more joyful.

May your days ahead be filled with the sweet aroma of these fruits, and may every step you take resonate with the love, wisdom, and grace of God. Our adventure may have concluded within these pages, but outside, in the vast expanse of life, a new, enriching chapter awaits. Here's to becoming the most fruitful explorers of our time!

Adventures in Scriptures

Other Books in the Series

If you enjoyed and found inspiration reading Exploring the Fruit of the Spirit, you won't want to miss the other captivating volumes in our series. Each book takes a deeper look into key biblical themes and virtues, offering a treasure trove of wisdom and guidance for your spiritual journey. From "Exploring the Armor of God" to the uplifting lessons in "Exploring the Parable Teachings of Jesus," our series is designed to nurture your soul, strengthen your faith, and light your path. Let's set out on this continuing adventure to discover more about love, grace, and the transformative power of faith. Let each page turn be a step closer to a deeper understanding and a fuller heart. Join us as we explore the riches of God's word and the endless beauty it holds for our lives.

1. Exploring the Fruit of the Spirit

2. Exploring the Armor of God

3. Exploring the Parable Teachings of Jesus

4. Exploring the Great Men of the Bible

5. Exploring the Great Women of the Bible

6. Exploring the Life of Jesus

We hope "Exploring the Fruit of the Spirit" has been a source of inspiration and growth on your spiritual journey. If this book has touched your heart, illuminated your path, or brought new insights into your life, we'd be honored if you would share your experience. Please take a moment to leave a review. Your feedback not only supports our work but also guides others in their quest for spiritual enrichment. Share how "Exploring the Fruit of the Spirit" has blessed you with a better understanding of the Fruit of the Spirit that it may inspire others on this journey of faith. Leave your review today and help spread the seeds of Love, Joy, Peace, and you know all the rest. Thank you for being a part of our community and for your invaluable contribution to this shared journey.

Biblical References Notices

NKJV

Scripture taken from the New King James Version®. Copyright © 1982 by Thomas Nelson. Used by permission. All rights reserved. All Scripture quotations

NIV

Scripture quotations marked (NIV) are taken from the Holy Bible, New International Version®, NIV®. Copyright © 1973, 1978, 1984, 2011 by Biblica, Inc.™ Used by permission of Zondervan. All rights reserved worldwide. www.zondervan.comThe "NIV" and "New International Version" are trademarks registered in the United States Patent and Trademark Office by Biblica, Inc.™

NLT

Scripture quotations marked (NLT) are taken from the Holy Bible, New Living Translation, copyright ©1996, 2004, 2015 by Tyndale House Foundation. Used by permission of Tyndale House Publishers, Carol Stream, Illinois 60188. All rights reserved.

www.ingramcontent.com/pod-product-compliance
Lightning Source LLC
Chambersburg PA
CBHW070915160726
48004CB00003B/1378